WHAT ABOUT THE CHURCH?

Booklets from *Questions of Life* include:

Is There More to Life Than This?

Who Is Jesus?

Why Did Jesus Die?

How Can We Have Faith?

Why and How Do I Pray?

Why and How Should I Read the Bible?

How Does God Guide Us?

The Holy Spirit

How Can I Resist Evil?

Why and How Should I Tell Others?

Does God Heal Today?

What about the Church?

How Can I Make the Most of the Rest of My Life?

WHAT ABOUT THE CHURCH?

NICKY GUMBEL

Alpha

Published in North America by Alpha North America
2275 Half Day Road, Suite 185, Deerfield, IL 60015

First published in 1993
Revised 2011

First printed by Alpha North America in 2007
Revised 2011

Printed in the United States of America

Cover and text illustrations by Charlie Mackesy

ISBN 978-1-933114-92-7

2 3 4 5 6 7 8 9 10 Printing/Year 14 13 12

CONTENTS

WHAT ABOUT THE CHURCH?

Abraham Lincoln once said, "If all the people who fell asleep in church on Sunday morning were laid out end to end . . . they would be a great deal more comfortable." Before I became a Christian my heart used to sink when I heard the word "church." The first thing that came to mind was church services: hard pews, unsingable tunes, enforced silences, and excruciating boredom. A vicar was taking a small boy around his church one day and showing him the memorials. "These are the names of those who died in the Services." The boy asked, "Did they die at the morning service or at the evening service?"

Some associate the word "church" with the clergy. Someone who is entering the ordained ministry is said to be "going into the church." Those embarking on such a career are often viewed with suspicion, and the assumption is made that they are absolutely incapable of doing anything else. Hence a recent advertisement it the church press: "Are you forty-five and going nowhere? Why not consider the Christian ministry?" Clergy are sometimes perceived as: "Six days invisible, one day incomprehensible!"

Others associate the word "church" with denominations. My mother, before she became a Christian, filled out a form that asked for her religion. She replied, "None (Church of England)!" Still others associate "church" with buildings. They assume that to be a clergyman you must be interested in church architecture, and when they go on holiday they send their vicar a picture of the local church building.

There may be an element of truth in some of these views. Yet these associations don't capture the essence of the church. It is similar to asking, "What is marriage?" and receiving the answer that marriage is a ring, a marriage certificate, a wedding service, and the marriage laws. Marriage may involve all of those things, but they are not the essence. At the heart of marriage is something far more profound—a relationship of trust based upon love and commitment. Similarly, at the heart of the church is something beautiful—the relationship between God and his people. Over the years since I have been a Christian, I have come not just to like the church but to love it.

In the New Testament there are over 100 images or analogies of the church. In this chapter I want to look at five, which are central to our understanding of the church.

The people of God

First, the church is people. The Greek word for church, *ekklesia*, means "an assembly" or "gathering of people." The Christian faith involves first of all a vertical relationship (our relationship with God) but also a horizontal relationship (our relationship with other people). We are part of a community that began with God's call to Abraham; the people of Israel prefigured the church. So the universal church consists of all those across the world and down the ages who profess or have professed the name of Christ.

Baptism is a visible mark of being a member of the church. It is also a visible sign of what it means to be a Christian. It signifies cleansing from sin (1 Corinthians 6:11), dying and rising with Christ to a new life (Romans 6:3-5; Colossians 2:12), and the living water which the Holy Spirit brings to our lives (1 Corinthians 12:13). Jesus Himself commanded His followers to go and make disciples and to baptize them (Matthew 28:19).

The universal Christian church is vast. According to the *Encyclopaedia Britannica* there are over two billion Christians in the world today, about a third of the world's population. Tens of thousands of people become Christians every day. Living in Western Europe, where the church has been in decline for many years, it is easy to think that the church is dying out. At one time, the West was sending missionaries out to other parts of the world. However, I remember that when I was in Cambridge, three Ugandan missionaries came there to preach the gospel. It struck me then how much the world had changed in the last 150 years, and that England needed missionaries as much as anywhere else.

Globally, the church is growing faster than ever. In 1900 there were 10 million Christians in Africa. One hundred years later there were 360 million. The same growth is evident in South America, China, and in various other parts of the world. In America about 50 per cent of the population goes to church on Sunday, compared with 7 percent in the U.K.

In more than sixty countries in the world the church is persecuted. More than 200 million Christians are harassed, abused, tortured, or executed on account of their faith, living in daily fear of secret police, vigilantes, or state repression and discrimination.[1] Yet the church in those parts of the world, by all accounts, remains very strong.

In the New Testament, Paul speaks of local churches, for example the "Galatian churches" (1 Corinthians 16:1), "the churches in the province of Asia" (1 Corinthians 16:19), and "all the churches of Christ" (Romans 16:16). Even those local churches themselves seem at times to have broken down into smaller gatherings which met in homes (Romans 16:5; 1 Corinthians 16:19).

In effect, there seem to have been three types of gathering in the Bible: the large, the medium-sized, and the small. These have been described as "celebration," "congregation," and "cell." In our experience as a local church all three are important and complement each other.

The celebration is a large gathering of Christians. This may take place every Sunday in big churches, or when a number of small churches come together for worship. In the Old Testament, the people of God came together for special celebrations with a festive atmosphere at Passover, Pentecost, or at the New Year. Today, large gatherings of Christians provide inspiration. Through them, many can recapture a vision of the greatness of God and a profound sense of worship. These gatherings of hundreds of Christians together can restore confidence to those who have felt isolated and provide a visible presence of the church in the community. However, on their own such gatherings are not enough. They are not places where friendships can easily develop.

The congregation, in this sense, is a medium-sized gathering. The size makes it possible to know most people. It is a place where lasting Christian friendships can be made. It is a place where individuals can learn, for example, to give talks, participate in worship, pray for the sick, participate in the liturgy and learn to pray out loud. It is also a place where the gifts and ministries of the Spirit, such as prophecy, can be exercised in an atmosphere of love and acceptance, where people are free to risk making mistakes. It is at this level that we can also go out as a group and serve our community. This could involve, for example, visiting the sick and elderly, painting the home of someone in need, or helping out at a homeless shelter or youth group.

The third level of meeting is the cell or small group. These groups consist of between two and twelve people, who gather to study the Bible and pray together. It is in these groups that the closest friendships in church are made. People are free to talk about their doubts, fears, and failures. We can encourage each other, eat together, and celebrate life's blessings. We can ask others to pray for us and be there for each other in difficult times. It should be a place of confidentiality, accountability, and respect.

The family of God

Second, the church is the family of God. When we receive Jesus Christ into our lives, we become children of God (John 1:12). This is what gives the church its unity. We have God as our Father, Jesus Christ as our Savior, and the Holy Spirit who lives within us. We all belong to one family. Although brothers and sisters may squabble and fall out or not see each other for long periods of time, they still remain brothers and sisters. Nothing can end that relationship. The church is one, even though it often appears to be divided.

This does not mean that we settle for disunity. Jesus prayed for His followers "that they may be one" (John 17:11). Paul says, "Make every effort to keep the unity of the Spirit" (Ephesians 4:3). Like a divided family we should always strive for reconciliation; our divisions are inevitably off-putting to those outside the church. Of course, unity should not be achieved at the expense of truth but, as the medieval writer Rupertus Meldenius put it, "On the necessary points, unity; on the questionable points, liberty; in everything, love."

At every level we should seek unity—in the small group, congregation, and celebration, and within our denomination and between denominations. This unity is brought about as theologians and church leaders get together to debate and work through theological differences. But it is also achieved, often more effectively, by ordinary Christians getting together to pray, worship, and work together. The nearer we come to Christ, the nearer we come to each other. David Watson, the writer and church leader, used a striking illustration. He said:

> When you travel by air and the plane lifts off the ground, the walls and hedges which may seem large and impressive at ground level, at once lose their significance. In the same way, when the power of the Holy Spirit lifts us up together into the conscious realization of the presence of Jesus, the barriers between us become unimportant. Seated with Christ in the heavenly places, the differences between Christians can often seem petty and marginal.[2]

Since we have the same Father, we are brothers and sisters and are all called to love one another. John puts it very clearly:

> If anyone says, "I love God," yet hates his brother, he is a liar. For anyone who does not love his brother, whom he has seen, cannot love God, whom he has not seen. And he has given us this command: Whoever loves God must also love his brother. Everyone who believes that Jesus is the Christ is born of God, and everyone who loves the father loves his child as well. (1 John 4:20–5:1)

Raniero Cantalamessa, addressing a gathering of thousands from many different denominations, said, "When Christians quarrel we say to God: 'Choose between us and them.' But the Father loves all His children. We should say, 'We accept as our brothers and sisters all those whom You receive as Your children.'"

We are called to fellowship with one another. The Greek word *koinonia* means "having in common" or "sharing." It is the word used for the marital relationship, the most intimate between human beings. Our fellowship is with God (Father, Son, and Holy Spirit—1 John 1:3; 2 Corinthians 13:14) and with one another (1 John 1:7). Christian fellowship cuts across race, color, education, background, and every other cultural barrier. There is a level of friendship in the church which I have certainly never experienced outside the church.

John Wesley said, "The New Testament knows nothing of solitary religion." We are called to fellowship with one another. It is not an optional extra. There are two things we simply cannot do alone. We cannot marry alone and we cannot be a Christian alone. Professor C. E. B. Cranfield put it like this, "The freelance Christian, who would be a Christian but is too superior to belong to the visible Church upon earth in one of its forms, is simply a contradiction in terms."

The writer of Hebrews urges his readers, "Let us consider how we may spur one another on towards love and good deeds. Let us not give up meeting together, as some are in the habit of doing, but let us encourage one another—and all the more as you see the Day approaching" (Hebrews 10:24-25). It is my experience of watching people who have come to Christ that unless they meet together with other Christians, it is difficult for their faith to stay alive.

One man who found himself in this position was visited by a wise old Christian. They sat in front of the coal fire in the sitting room. The old man never spoke, but went to the coal fire and picked out a red-hot coal with some tongs and put it on the hearth. He still said nothing. In a few minutes the coal had lost its glow. Then he picked it up and put it back in the fire. After a short time it began to glow again. The old man still said nothing at all but, as he got up to leave, the other man knew exactly why he had lost his fervor—a Christian out of fellowship is like a coal out of the fire.

A young couple who had recently come to faith in Christ wrote:

> We have been coming to church for a year now and it already feels like home. The atmosphere of love, friendship, and excitement is impossible to find elsewhere. The joy of it far exceeds any evening at a pub, party, or restaurant . . . I am shocked to say (although I continue to enjoy all three!) Both of us find that Sunday's services and Wednesday's gatherings are two high points of the week. At times, it feels like coming up for air, especially as by Wednesday it is to be drowning in the deep waters of working life! If we miss either, we feel somehow "diluted." Of course, we can keep talking to God together and alone, but I feel that the act of meeting together is the bellows that keep on fanning the flames of our faith.

The body of Christ

Third, the church is the body of Christ. Paul had been persecuting the Christian church when he encountered Jesus Christ on the road to Damascus. Jesus said to him, "Saul, Saul, why do you persecute *me*?" (Acts 9:4, italics mine). Paul had never met Jesus before so he must have realized that Jesus was saying that, in persecuting Christians, he was persecuting Jesus Himself. It may well be that from his encounter Paul realized that the church was the body of Christ. "He calls the church Christ," wrote the sixteenth-century reformer, Calvin. We Christians are Christ to the world. As the old hymn says:

> He has no hands but our hands
> To do His work today;
> He has no feet but our feet
> To lead men in His way;
> He has no voice but our voice
> To tell men how He died;
> He has no help but our help
> To lead them to His side.

Paul develops this analogy in 1 Corinthians 12. The body is a unit (v. 12), yet this unity does not mean uniformity. Within the body there is almost infinite variety. People have different gifts and serve in different ways, but everybody fits in somewhere. God gives each of us a role in the church, not so we can show off, but for the common good (v. 7). If we don't play our part the whole body suffers. In this sense the church has been compared to a football game: twenty-two people desperately in need of a rest, being watched by twenty-two thousand people desperately in need of exercise. Each one of us represents Jesus and can do His good deeds wherever we go: in our families, at work, where we live, and with our friends.

John Wimber was once approached by a member of his congregation who had met somebody in great need. After the Sunday service this man told John Wimber of his frustration in trying to get help, "This man needed a place to stay, food, and support while he gets on his feet and looks for a job. I am really frustrated. I tried telephoning the church office, but no one could see me and they couldn't help me. I finally ended up having to let him stay with *me* for the week! Don't you think the church should take care of people like this?" John Wimber thought for a moment and then said, "It looks like *the church* did."

What should our attitude be to other parts of the body of Christ? Paul deals with two wrong attitudes.

First, he speaks to those who feel inferior and who feel that they have nothing to offer. For example, Paul says the foot may feel inferior to the hand or the ear inferior to the eye (vv. 14-19). It is a human tendency to feel envious of others.

It is easy to look round the church and feel inferior and therefore not needed. As a result we do nothing. In fact, we are all needed. God has given gifts "to each one" (v. 7). The term "to each one" runs through 1 Corinthians 12 as a common thread. Each person has at least one gift that is absolutely necessary for the proper functioning of the body. Unless each of us plays the part God has designed for us, the church will not be able to function as it should.

In the following verses, Paul turns to those who feel superior (vv. 21-25) and are saying to others, "I don't need you." Again, Paul points out the folly of this position. A body without a foot is not as effective as it might be (see v. 21). Often the parts that are unseen are even more important than those with a higher profile.

We need to recognize that we are all in it together; there is a mutual dependence, and each part affects the whole: "If one part suffers, every part suffers with it; if one part is honored, every part rejoices with it" (v. 26). When everybody is playing their part something really beautiful occurs, like an orchestra where many people are performing. Globally as well, this is true. Rather than dismissing other parts of the church because they are different from us, it is exciting to realize that we can be enriched by them.

A holy temple

Fourth, in the church we experience the presence of God. The only church building the New Testament speaks about is a building made of people. Paul says that the Christians are "being built together to become a dwelling in which God lives by his Spirit" (Ephesians 2:22). Jesus is the chief cornerstone. He is the one who founded the church and around whom the church is built. The foundations are "the apostles and prophets" and the result is a holy temple made of "living stones."

In the Old Testament the tabernacle (and later the temple) was central to Israel's worship. This was the place where people went to meet with God. At times His presence filled the temple (1 Kings 8:11) and especially the Holy of Holies. Access to His presence was strictly limited (see Hebrews 9).

Through His death on the cross for us, Jesus opened up access to the Father for all believers all the time. His presence is no longer confined to a physical temple; now He is present by His Spirit with all believers. His presence is especially sensed when Christians gather together (Matthew 18:20). His new temple is the church, which is "a dwelling in which God lives by his Spirit."

Professor Gordon Fee writes that presence "is a delicious word." If you love someone, what you want more than anything else is that person's presence. Letters are good; photos are great; telephone calls are fantastic. But what you really long for is their presence.[3] The presence of God was what Adam and Eve lost in the Garden of Eden. But God promised that He would restore His presence. First in the temple in the Old Testament and after Pentecost, when the Spirit of God was poured out, the presence of God came to live among His people.

Paul writes of individual Christians, "Do you not know that your bodies are temples of the Holy Spirit, who is in you, whom you have received from God?" (1 Corinthians 6:19). But more often he writes that the church, the gathered community of Christians, is the temple of the Holy Spirit. That is where God lives by His Spirit. Under the Old Covenant (before Jesus), access to the Father was through a priest (Hebrews 4:14), who made sacrifices on behalf of believers. Now Jesus, our great high priest, has made the supreme sacrifice of His own life on our behalf. Jesus "appeared once for all at the end of the ages to do away with sin by the sacrifice of himself" (Hebrews 9:26). We do not need to make further sacrifices for our sins. Rather, we need to be constantly reminded of His sacrifice for us. At the service of Holy Communion, sometimes called the Lord's Supper or the Eucharist, we remember His sacrifice with thanksgiving and partake of its benefits.

As we receive the bread and wine we look in four directions:

We look back with thanks
The bread and wine remind us of the broken body and shed blood of Jesus Christ on the cross. As we receive Communion we look back to the cross with thankfulness that He died for us so that our sins could be forgiven and our guilt removed (Matthew 26:26-28).

We look forward with anticipation
Jesus could have left us some other way to remember His death, but He chose to leave us a meal. A meal is

often a way in which we celebrate great occasions. One day in heaven we are going to celebrate for eternity at "the wedding supper" of Jesus Christ (Revelation 19:9). The bread and wine are a foretaste of this (Luke 22:16; 1 Corinthians 11:26).

We look around at the Christian family

Drinking from one cup and eating the one loaf symbolizes our unity in Christ. "Because there is one loaf, we, who are many, are one body, for we all partake of the one loaf" (1 Corinthians 10:17). That is why we do not receive the bread and the wine on our own. Eating and drinking together in this way should not only remind us of our unity, it should strengthen that unity as we look around at our brothers and sisters for whom Christ died.

We look up in expectation

The bread and wine represent the body and blood of Jesus. Jesus promised to be with us by His Spirit after His death, and especially wherever Christians meet together: "Where two or three come together in my name, there am I with them" (Matthew 18:20). So as we receive Communion we look up to Jesus with expectancy. In our experience, we have found that on such occasions there are sometimes conversions, healing, and powerful encounters with the presence of Christ.

The bride of Christ

Fifth, Jesus loves the church; it is the bride of Christ. This is one of the most beautiful analogies of the church in the New Testament. Paul says, when speaking of the husband and wife relationship: "This is a profound mystery—but I am talking about Christ and the church" (Ephesians 5:32).

To describe the relationship between God and human beings the New Testament uses analogies of the closest possible relationship. A prominent analogy, for example, is that of a parent to a child. Yet here Paul suggests that perhaps the best analogy is that of the love between a husband and a wife. That is the love that Jesus has for you. St. Augustine said, "God loves each one of us as if there was only one of us to love."

As the Old Testament speaks about God being a husband to Israel (Isaiah 54:1-8), so in the New Testament Paul speaks about Christ being a husband to the church and the model of every human marriage relationship. So he tells husbands to love their wives "just as Christ loved the church and gave himself up for her to make her holy, cleansing her by the washing with water through the word, and to present her to himself as a radiant church, without stain or wrinkle or any other blemish, but holy and blameless" (Ephesians 5:25-27).

This picture of the holy and radiant church may not entirely reflect its present condition, but we get a glimpse here of what Jesus intends for His church. One day Jesus will return in glory. In the Book of Revelation, John has a vision of the church, "the new Jerusalem, coming down out of heaven from God, prepared as a bride beautifully dressed for her husband" (Revelation 21:2). Today the church is small and weak. One day we shall see the church as Jesus intends it to be. In the meantime, we must try to bring our experiences as close as possible to the vision of the New Testament.

Our response to Christ's love for us should be one of love for Him. The way we show our love for Him is by living in holiness and purity—being a bride fit for Him and fulfilling His purpose for us. This is His intention for us. This is how His purposes for us will be fulfilled. We are to be changed and to be made beautiful until we are fit to be His bride.

Jackie Pullinger, whom I have mentioned before, works particularly with heroin addicts and prostitutes in Hong Kong. Jackie met a seventy-two-year-old woman named Alfreda who had been a heroin addict and a prostitute for sixty years. When Jackie met her she used to sit outside a brothel all day in a run-down area of the city. She would inject heroin into her back three times a day, her legs and her arms having been overused. Without an identity card, as far as the Hong Kong government was concerned, she didn't even exist. She gave her life to Christ and she received forgiveness. She went to live in one of Jackie's houses and as God healed her she began to change.

Later, she met a man called Little Wa, who was seventy-five, and they got married. Jackie described their wedding as "the wedding of the decade" because Alfreda, a former prostitute and heroin addict, walked down the aisle in white, cleansed, forgiven, and transformed by the love of Jesus Christ. To me this is a picture of the church. There is only one way into the church, and that is to say, "God, be merciful to me, a sinner." When we say that, God in His love responds, "You are part of My people. You are My family. You are My representative; you are My body on earth. You are a holy temple; My Spirit lives within you. You are My bride."

ENDNOTES

1. The degree and location of Christian persecution around the world is continually changing. For more information and details on how to support and pray for this part of the church see, for example, www. opendoorsuk.org

2. David Watson, *I Believe in the Church* (Hodder & Stoughton, 1978).

3. Gordon Fee, *Paul, The Spirit and the People of God* (Hodder & Stoughton, 1997).

ALPHA

This book is an Alpha resource. The Alpha course is a practical introduction to the Christian faith initiated by Holy Trinity Brompton in London, and now being run by thousands of churches throughout the U.K. and North America, and internationally.

For more information on Alpha, and details of available resources, please contact:

Alpha U.S.A.
2275 Half Day Road
Suite 185
Deerfield, IL 60015
Tel: 800.362.5742
Tel: + 212.406.5269
e-mail: info@alphausa.org
www.alphausa.org

Alpha in the Caribbean
Holy Trinity Brompton
Brompton Road
London SW7 1JA UK
Tel: +44 (0) 845.644.7544
e-mail: americas@alpha.org
www.alpha.org

Alpha Canada
Suite #230 – 11331 Coppersmith Way
Riverside Business Park
Richmond, BC V7A 5J9
Tel: 800.743.0899
Fax: 604.271.6124
e-mail: office@alphacanada.org
www.alphacanada.org

To purchase resources in Canada:

David C. Cook Distribution Canada
P.O. Box 98, 55 Woodslee Avenue
Paris, ON N3L 3E5
Tel: 800.263.2664
Fax: 800.461.8575
e-mail: custserve@davidccook.ca
www.davidccook.ca

ALPHA BOOKS

Why Jesus? (20072) A booklet given to all participants at the start of the Alpha course. "The clearest, best illustrated and most challenging short presentation of Jesus that I know."

—Michael Green

Why Christmas? / Why Easter? (20081, 20075) The Christmas and Easter versions of Why Jesus?

Questions of Life (105021) The Alpha course in book form. In fifteen compelling chapters Nicky Gumbel points the way to an authentic Christianity which is exciting and relevant to the world today.

Searching Issues (105023) The seven issues most often raised by participants on the Alpha course: suffering, other religions, sex before marriage, the New Age, homosexuality, science and Christianity, and the Trinity.

A Life Worth Living (105024) What happens after Alpha? Based on the book of Philippians, this is an invaluable next step for those who have just completed the Alpha course, and for anyone eager to put their faith on a firm biblical footing.

How to Run the Alpha Course: Telling Others (16620)
The theological principles and the practical details of
how courses are run. Each alternate chapter consists
of a testimony of someone whose life has been
changed by God through an Alpha course.

The Jesus Lifestyle (25327) Studies in the Sermon on
the Mount showing how Jesus' teaching flies in
the face of modern lifestyle and presents us with a
radical alternative.

30 Days (54057) Nicky Gumbel selects thirty passages
from the Old and New Testament which can be read
over thirty days. It is designed for those on an Alpha
course and others who are interested in beginning to
explore the Bible.

The Heart of Revival (52884) Ten Bible studies based
on the book of Isaiah, drawing out important truths
for today by interpreting some of the teaching of the
Old Testament prophet Isaiah. The book seeks to
understand what revival might mean and how we
can prepare to be part of it.

*All titles are by Nicky Gumbel, who is the Vicar of
Holy Trinity Brompton in London*

NOTES

NOTES

NOTES